Thursdays With Mom

A collection of true and heartwarming experiences during my time as a caregiver for my mother when she was in her 80s and battling dementia. The invaluable lesson I learned is that, while much of life is beyond our control, we can choose our perspective and find the goodness in it.

By Susan M. Daniel

Copyright

Copyright © 2025 Susan M Daniel

Published by

All rights reserved. No part of this book may be reproduced or transmitted in any form or by any means, electronic or mechanical, including photocopying, recording, or using any information storage and retrieval system, without the written permission of the publisher and author.

"It is only with the heart that one can see rightly: what is essential is invisible to the eye."

-Antoine de Saint-Exupery, "The Little Prince

Dedication

This book is dedicated to my siblings, Jane, Tom, and Holly, who were right there with me during the caregiving journey. They made many trips back home to assist with care and offer support, sharing bittersweet memories along the way. No caregiver should go it alone...how very fortunate I was to have them by my side.

Table of Contents

Prologue 7

What's the Hurry? 11

The Price of Shrimp is Going Up - The Whole World is Screwed Up 13

Gone in 60 Seconds 17

Quote of the Day 21

Great Expectations 23

"I'll Show You Dr. R" 27

FAQ's 31

Who Came Up with That Idea?? 35

You Come Here Often? 39

Dear Santa 41

Quote of the Week 43

Sweet Grandma. Sweet, Sweet, Sweet Grandma 45

Value is Relative 47

Will I Ever Learn My Lesson? 51

Grandma on Gatorade 55

A Day with Mom 59

Which Side of the Coin? 63

Lordy, Lordy! Grandma Thinks She's 40!.... 67

Can You Ring Me Up?... 71

Step, Hop, Step, Hop.. 75

The Rain in Spain Stay Mainly In The Plain 79

Does The End Justify The Means? 83

'Tis Good To Laugh At Oneself..................... 87

A New Car!! A New Day!! 91

Let It Go, Let It Go 95

Groceries With Grandma 99

It's Good To Be Back 105

The Truth Serum..109

White Or Rye? 113

Great Grandmother, Great Granddaughter, Great Scott!.. 117

The Best Laid Plans… 121

Mom..125

Prologue

The Background

Our mom had the biggest heart. She was happiest when she was helping someone—whether it was giving a neighbor a ride, letting my son borrow her car, hemming my pants, or rallying behind a cause that a friend believed in. You could not enter her home without being offered a sandwich, coffee, chocolate, wine—whatever she had.

Our mom was a hoot! She loved a party, joined in on anything that looked like fun, and always took it to the next level. She and Dad hosted themed parties, attended every happy hour, organized boat parades, and were often the life of the party. She taught us to "go for it," encouraging us to try whatever our hearts desired and never miss an opportunity.

Our mom was adventurous. She discovered a love for travel as a single woman in her 20s. Her happy place was the Jack and Jill Ranch in Michigan, where she would spend summers with friends, dress like a cowgirl, and ride horses. She was an excellent ice skater, a talented seamstress, and always a classy dresser—usually with a large hat, but never anything too "prissy."

Mom loved our father and all four of us children. She loved dogs and horses and had a soft spot for the "weak." She taught us that we were not better than anyone else, and that no one was better than we were. She judged people by what was in their hearts. Her favorite quote, from her beloved book "The Little Prince," was: "It is only with the heart that one can see rightly. What is essential is invisible to the eye."

Dementia took so much of our mom away. Though she was never officially diagnosed, it came on slowly—at first, confusing words, which we found funny, but only frustrated her. It became more obvious as she forgot to pay bills, sometimes leading to canceled credit cards or insurance—infuriating for her, as she had always been diligent. Then came the repetitions: telling the same story so often it challenged our patience to listen and laugh one more time. The doctor finally supported us when Mom started confusing her medications, refusing to take them, or taking the wrong ones.

I became Mom's primary caregiver. Dad had passed away several years earlier, and Mom eventually moved back to our hometown, where I lived. I took responsibility for doctors' visits, managing finances, and taking her out on Thursdays for lunch, shopping, and errands—tasks I was glad to do. The problem was that Mom insisted she didn't need any help from anyone. She resisted any involvement with her bills or paperwork. She became angry, believing the doctor was telling me things he wasn't telling her, as she was unable to process his information quickly. She was indignant at the idea of relying on me or my brother and sisters for assistance. As her health continued to fail, she adamantly refused to accept the idea of aging or any suggestion of incompetence.

Dementia was bringing out an anger and bitterness in our mom, mad at the world for what was happening to her. She became tough, as logic seemed to disappear. I later learned that the one closest to her—me—bore the brunt of her anger. I was often frustrated beyond control as I watched her suffer because she refused my help with medications. I had to sneak behind her back to pay her bills, trying to prevent further cancellations; she had already lost her health insurance, electricity, cable TV, and more. She complained, ranted, and became unpleasant to be around. This was not our mother.

As things worsened, I grew stressed and frustrated to an unhealthy degree, bringing that negativity home. No one wanted to listen to me complain, and I couldn't blame them. But I needed help. I finally joined a caregiver support group, where I came to realize that I wasn't going to change Mom's behavior—she couldn't help what had taken over her mind. I had to change how I dealt with Mom, and with my own feelings. I found relief knowing that I was not alone; so many others shared similar struggles.

I had quit my full-time job to become her caregiver. I wanted to keep the family updated on Mom's health and activities, but I did not want to keep sending troubling news. I realized that, throughout each day with Mom, glimpses of her funny, generous side still appeared. That's what my family needed to hear. So, I started a blog to share the funny, sweet, and endearing events of our times. The family looked so forward to my stories, which brought them comfort and laughter amidst a rather unsettling period.

I am sharing this in the hope that it reaches someone who needs it and brings a few smiles to all.

What's the Hurry?

March 2010

Set the Scene: Mom loved Happy Hour. 5:00 p.m. meant she could enjoy her cherished Manhattan. It used to be the revered Martini, until one year Mom and Dad gave up Martinis for Lent and substituted Manhattan...they never went back. Mom also loved cutting articles out of the newspaper that she thought were relevant to our lives and mailing them to us. Of course, with the internet, we had probably already seen that "news," but it was still nice to know she was thinking of us.

Spring Forward! Okay, honestly, no one wants to lose that extra hour of sleep on a Sunday morning in early spring.

Yet for reasons still not fully explained, Mom set her clocks forward one hour on Friday night instead of waiting with everyone else to change the time on Saturday night. Was it because she didn't want to forget? Or had she already forgotten that it was Friday and not Saturday? Or was she anxious about having one more hour of daylight for driving before it got dark? I'm not sure, especially since she had already given me my own personal, cut-out copy of the newspaper article reminding me to change the time (thanks, Mom!). I think she wanted to make sure I wouldn't miss Mass on Sunday.

Oh well, Sunday morning came just the same. The bonus was that Happy Hour arrived an hour earlier!

Lesson Learned: Patience is a virtue for any caregiver. Why become frustrated over insignificant mishaps that don't hurt anyone? Often, our worry is rooted in the fear that these little acts might become more serious issues... but most are beyond our control. "Save it for the big stuff."

The Price of Shrimp is Going Up - The Whole World is Screwed Up

May 2010

Set the Scene: The trips to the grocery store became very long. Before Mom moved back to our hometown, she and Dad lived in a small town in Michigan and shopped at the local mom-and-pop grocery. Now, she found herself overwhelmed by the number of choices available and had difficulty making decisions. The store was too big, the technology was confusing, and everything seemed complicated. At the end of the day, she would find comfort in the familiarity of her beloved news on TV. She was a self-proclaimed Fox "news junkie" and followed Bill O'Reilly religiously.

Very eloquently put, Mom. But you're right—things are often out of control. A trip to the grocery store becomes overwhelming because there are about 20 versions of Tide to choose from, 50 types of fruit juice, and you have to use your Kroger card to save on gas—if you can figure out all the steps to get the discount at the pump. While you're there, the cell phone is buzzing... is someone calling you? Texting you? Or is it simply warning you that the battery is low because you didn't charge it, even though you've hardly used it?

A visit to the great-granddaughter puts things a little more in perspective. A new, innocent, curious mind investigating life from a different point of view. Little hands grab dirt from a plant and scatter it across the carpet... great-grandma's response? "Oh crap!" The 14-year-old grandson's reaction to his grandma—eyebrows raised, muffling a shocked, amused laugh—"Did I really hear that?!?"

It's good to go home to the comforts of the familiar. Turn on the news and see what they've messed up now. Mom was disturbed by the report of an oil spill in the Gulf of Mexico... "Red Lobster is really going to suffer—the price of shrimp will go up!" You're right again, Mom. This world is screwed up. Moving too fast, too many choices, and nobody has time for anyone else.

To hell with it! There's nothing wrong with spending an evening with Bill O'Reilly and a Manhattan. Besides, it's hard to find someone who knows how to make a good Manhattan!

Lesson Learned: Slow down. We can't expect someone a few decades older than us to keep up with our pace, any more than we can keep up with our grandchildren's energy level. We need to put ourselves in their shoes—tackle one thing at a time and take time to smell the roses along the way. Besides, they need something to look forward to tomorrow.

Gone in 60 Seconds...

May 2010

Set the Scene: For some reason, Mom always felt the need to pick up every free brochure she came across. They could be travel brochures, how-to pamphlets, medical advice—whatever. And she never threw them away. Mom loved a good cup of coffee. It was funny how long she could make one cup last. But her true weakness was sweets—donuts, chocolate, raspberry pie, just to name a few. Then she found the perfect combo...

Yep. Mom discovered the Mocha Frappuccino at Starbucks. She sucked it down so fast, only pausing several times briefly to say, "Boy, is this good!" As luck would have it, Starbucks was running a promotion: the Frappuccino was half-price for one week during their "Happy Hour" from 3 to 5 p.m. Well, you've got to try the special....

Besides, it was the end of a long day. A trip to Home Depot in search of a flower planter ended with a detour to the paint department to look at color chips. I failed to warn the helpful Home Depot paint guy who suggested we check out the Martha Stewart colors because they were so well coordinated. He had no idea... "That Martha Stewart paint surely has to be too pricey." After all, who can afford Martha Stewart? Well, we definitely got our money's worth — paint chips, paint brochures, paint how-to books, whatever print material we could take home for free.

Well, got to go. Mom just found an article in the paper about free shredding day in the local township—one day only, coming up in a couple of weeks. Boy, do we have our work cut out for us! Can't take a chance on missing this one!
- Gas round trip to Colerain for free shredding day: $20.00
- Price to have huge stacks of papers shredded: $0.00
- 'Putting a dent' in the many piles of papers at Mom's place: Priceless!

Lesson learned: A productive day doesn't always have to mean crossing items off your to-do list. Sometimes, it's about experiencing something new, opening your mind to possibilities, or simply taking pleasure in the little things.

Quote of the Day

May 2010

Set the Scene: Mom had false teeth, and she was not ashamed to admit it. When she came to stay with us from time to time, the grandkids never missed a chance to watch Grandma take her teeth out and scrub them each morning. She also loved a bargain.

Here it is...

"I have a second set of teeth at home in the drawer."

The best part (!)...

"I got them for half price!!!"

Enough said...

Lesson learned: Our inhibitions build protective walls around us. Why worry about what others might think? Being open and honest with ourselves and with others makes us more "real"—more approachable, less uptight, and more genuine. Go ahead—let your guard down!

Great Expectations

May 2010

Set the Scene: Mom was struggling with COPD, brought on by years of smoking, which made walking even a short distance difficult. She was convinced that the doctor could "just fix it" and that she would be able to return to her favorite sports—ice skating and horseback riding. She was in denial about her body aging and was determined to fight it with everything she had.

Optimism is admirable. Both Mom and Dad epitomized positive thinking—a wonderful way to shield us, and themselves, from the realities of the world. However, we all have to face reality eventually. I give Mom credit for wanting to get back to the gym. However, I struggled to convince her that joining the new Cycling Class was not in her best interest. Sometimes, it takes an outsider to break the news.

The recent doctor visit was a harsh dose of reality. The ever-gracious and patient doctor answered all our questions, some of them multiple times(!). Mom asked if her breathing would get better if she exercised. His first answer was a thorough explanation about how our bodies' capabilities diminish with age, though exercise could help "a little bit." She then asked, "Should I walk or jog?" The doctor replied, "I don't think I'll see you jogging!" She asked a second time, telling him she had been active in horseback riding, swimming, and ice skating—up until a couple of years ago(!) I chimed in, making sure the doctor knew, "Mom, that was more than 50 years ago." The doctor still replied, "A little bit." The third time, Mom asked (no kidding!), "Will I be able to get on skates again?" The doctor snickered. When she repeated the question, he looked at me with a glance that said, "Is she kidding?" He knew it was time for honesty. He put his hand on her shoulder and said, "No more skating, for several reasons—including that you don't want to fall and break a bone."

Mom was finally satisfied. Now, she's trying to decide whether to take the Yoga class or the

Pilates class. Honestly, either is fine with me, since I might actually be able to keep up!

Lesson learned: Yes, we all slow down—some of us more quickly than others. But that doesn't mean we should give up. We need to keep going the best way we can, making adjustments and taking a different path. And always—stay positive!

"I'll Show You Dr. R"

June 2010

Set the Scene: Our parents' generation revered their doctors. They wouldn't dare question them or insult them by seeking a second opinion. However, they did expect doctors to maintain the professional image they associated with them. The "god" of all doctors to our mom was the well-known TV personality, Dr. Oz.

I knew Mom wasn't too fond of her own doctor. She didn't appreciate the way he sometimes responded to her questions in an almost cynical tone. She did mention, however, that he was a rather good-looking guy. Yet she found it odd that he wore "kiddy pajamas," referring to his bright-printed scrubs.

Needless to say, Mom was not looking forward to giving "Dr. R" the honor of performing her hand surgery. But since he came highly recommended, she agreed to go forward. She read the pre-op instructions a dozen times and struggled with deciding which pillow to bring for the ride home. The instructions said to wear "comfortable, loose clothing," but I was not prepared for Mom's take on that point...

When I went to pick Mom up for the big day, the first thing I noticed was a large hole in the front of the white pants she was wearing. "Mom, those pants have a big hole in them!" I had to tell her, wanting to shield her from embarrassment later and avoid adding more anxiety to the day. "We've got to take you shopping and get some new white pants."

She was neither surprised nor embarrassed. "Oh, I have nicer pants, but I'm not going to waste them on him. I figure if he can wear his pajamas, then I can wear my pants with a hole!". It's a shame that the wonderful Dr. Oz wasn't available for this hand surgery. I wonder what she would have worn for him?

Lesson Learned: Never let anyone treat you poorly or condescendingly, no matter their status. We might anger them by standing up for ourselves, but at least we gain their respect—and, more importantly, our own self-respect.

FAQ's

June 2010

Set the Scene: Mom loved a social outing, especially going out to lunch. It had to be a place that offered table service—no fast food, no "picnic ware" (i.e., plastic utensils), and a patient server was a must. She was willing to go anywhere, as long as it met her criteria. Once there, the menu always seemed overwhelming, but thanks to our weekly lunch outings, I learned well what Mom liked and disliked. Still, there were always extra requirements: the tomato had to be red (not whitish), the lettuce had to be something other than leaf lettuce, the bread couldn't be thick or hard, the fries absolutely had to be hot, and burgers were only acceptable if they were thin. Most importantly, the Manhattan had to be served "up," not "on the rocks"—otherwise, it was sent back.

In case you plan to spend any amount of time with Mom in the near future, you might appreciate this reference to FAQ's (Frequently Asked Questions).

Q: "Mom, are you ready to go to the grocery?"

A: "Let's get lunch."

Q: "Mom, would you like me to take you shopping for the household items you've been wanting?"

A: "Have you had lunch yet?"

Q: "I'll pick you up at 1:00 for the Doctor's appointment, then we can go back to your place and work on the mail and files, if you're up for that today?"

A: "Are you hungry?

You might see a pattern here. If you decide to go out to lunch, a few "guidelines" can help make it simple:

1. You will need to pick the place.
2. You will need to suggest what Mom might like to eat.
3. If it's late enough in the afternoon, be prepared to order a drink so Mom feels comfortable ordering her Manhattan.

4. Be ready to ask for a take-out container—leftovers are guaranteed (except for the Manhattan).

5. On the way home, she may want to stop for a hot fudge sundae.

Yes, I'm gaining weight, but Mom isn't. Now, how does that happen?

Lesson learned: Life's too short not to make the most of every day. Why settle for spending a day doing things that don't add to your joy? Somehow, the things that need to get done are still getting done, and happy times create great memories.

Who Came Up with That Idea??

August 2010

Set the Scene: Mom and Dad decided not to get a computer because they believed the internet was "evil and addicting." Everything was becoming much too complicated—cell phones replacing landlines, TVs with perplexing remotes, and sophisticated stereos taking the place of simple radios. I became the "go-to" person for operational needs, reassuring Mom that there was no reason to feel embarrassed.

How do we compete—or even survive—in a world that has advanced faster than our skin has aged? While we're busy raising kids, keeping up the house, and trying to remember the grandkids' birthdays, someone keeps coming up with new ways to improve technology.

Mom has a Hi-Def TV with all the channels you could ever want and picture-perfect quality, but she thought the cable bill was too expensive! A house call from the cable guy brought the bill down by $50 without compromising the five coveted channels she considered "crucial." Besides, Hi-Def seemed irrelevant to her.

Then the Bose CD player stopped working. Luckily, I was there to prevent a trip to Radio Shack to "check it out."

Mom's suggestion: "I think it needs a new needle."
"Mom, a CD works by a light reading tiny indentations on the disc."
"Then let's get a new light bulb!"

Oh! Save me! I checked the manual, pressed a few buttons on the remote, and bingo! I became the new hero!

Now, if only I could keep up with my kids' techno-gadgets and be their hero too...

Lesson learned: We might sigh at what seems like ineptness on someone else's part, but we'd better remember that soon enough, it will be us. We may have mastered our current technology, but cell phones and TVs will keep evolving into seemingly foreign devices. Be nice to those grandkids, we're going to depend on them someday!

You Come Here Often?

August 2010

Set the Scene: Mom never passed up a chance to get a discount, whether it was a 30-cent coupon or a BOGO deal—regardless of whether she needed it or not. Collecting frequent buyer cards from every establishment became a must! And you never know where you might go when you're "out and about," so it's best to bring them all along...

You know you've truly become a local when you have a collection of frequent shopper cards from every area retailer. Mom now has her own "My Panera" card. She also has a "Star Car Wash" buy-five-washes-get-one-free card. She keeps these in her wallet next to the "Kenning Circle K" dining card, the "Best Buy Reward Zone" card, and numerous others from all the local shops. Now, we just have to figure out how to get the wallet to close. Then, there's the challenge of fitting the wallet into the petite-sized purse Mom insists on carrying to match her petite stature. Of course, every time she needs to switch purses to coordinate with her shoes, she has to transfer all the coupons, papers, and frequent-whatever cards, often leaving no room for less significant items—like keys(!).

Good thing I have a copy of the house key. I've used it numerous times to unlock the door while Mom searches through her "huge" purse to locate her keys, as well as the credit card she used at the last stop. I've never taken the liberty of going through her purse—who knows what I might find...

Lesson Learned: It's good to have someone's back, especially when you know they need it. But, most importantly, never let them think you're one step ahead. Helping out while allowing them "save face" is a win-win—they maintain their dignity, and your life gets a little easier.

Dear Santa

September 2010

Set the Scene: Mom was a collector of all things that might someday have a purpose. We gave up long ago trying to convince her to part with the multitude of items that mostly created clutter and gathered dust. And yet, there are still some things she longed for...

There are 86 days until Christmas. And it will take me that long to figure out what to get Mom this year! However, I do know what Mom does not need for Christmas:
- pens
- pencils
- coffee mugs
- stuffed animals
- books on travel
- cookbooks
- small reused plastic storage containers
- knick-knacks

Now, if you find yourself at a real loss for ideas, here are a few things Mom mentioned she would actually like:

- a convertible
- Clark candy bars
- Obama out of office
- a 'cleared off' dining room table
- The Dr. Oz show back at its original time
- Jay's potato chips, which are not available in Cincinnati

And you thought your kids' Christmas lists were tough!

Lesson Learned: So, what if there are stacks of things that seem like useless clutter? If they are not causing any harm, forcing someone to let go of them might actually do more harm. Value is often personal, and who are we to decide what brings someone else joy?

Quote of the Week

March 2011

Set the Scene: One of the most difficult tasks for an adult child is to "take the keys"—convincing their aging parent that it's time to stop driving. We were fortunate to have "circumstances" that helped us do this difficult job.

The move from Michigan to Ohio required us to change Mom's auto insurance. We knew this might also mean needing to update her driver's license. The dreaded letter finally arrived last week, requesting her current "Ohio Driver's License Number." We both felt the heavy weight of the impending doom that comes with trying to pass a driving test at age 84 (although, admittedly, it could have been a blessing in disguise!). Mom had just one request, which quickly became the quote of the week:

"If I have to take a driving test, can I borrow someone's car? Because I can't see out of mine!"

One word of caution: if you see a large silver Cadillac with a few dents in the rear and an almost invisible driver—RUN!

Lesson Learned: Giving up one's independence must feel like giving up their last hope. When the time comes for the "tough love", we must remember that we are acting out of love. Our parents did it for us when we were young; now it's our turn to do the same for them.

Sweet Grandma. Sweet, Sweet, Sweet Grandma

March 2011

Set the Scene: As mentioned earlier, Mom loved sweets! Being as generous as she was, she assumed everyone loved them just as much as she did.

We all have our weaknesses—our Achilles' heel, our guilty pleasures. But we tend to keep them secret, so no one tries to stop us from indulging ourselves, even if it isn't the healthiest choice.

So...on a recent errand with Mom, she mentioned wanting to stop at the "pastry store" (the local bakery) on the way home to pick up some treats for me and the kids, knowing my son shares her love for doughnuts and Danish. I assured her we didn't need any of those "bad things." However, she insisted, and I gave in, knowing it made her feel good to give. Once inside, Mom hurried to the counter, eyes wide. "I'll have one of those," she said, pointing to the

Bear Claws. "Two of those," meaning the cherry-filled Danish. "A couple of these, a few of those…" "Mom!" I tried to interrupt. "That's way too much! We'll never eat that many!" She wouldn't let me stop her. Then, with a bag already full, she finally turned to me and said, "Okay, now pick out some for you and the kids." WHAT?! Mom—those were just for you?!

Oh, what goes on behind closed doors. Why do I put such effort into finding healthy restaurants to make sure Mom gets proper nutrition? Now I know why she hardly eats when we're out—she's full of jelly doughnuts and pecan wheels. Yet, if life's simple pleasures bring happiness, then bring 'em on!

Lesson Learned: Try as we might, we only have so much control over someone else's choices. We can guide, protect, and advise, but at the end of the day, whatever brings them happiness outweighs what we think is "best" for them.

Value is Relative

April 2011

Set the Scene: Mom somehow felt a very strong need to donate to every single charity request that came her way. At tax time, she would hand over the daunting, long list of recipients she had given to that year. Needless to say, some donations were questionable...

Ahhhh, tax time! The moment we face the fruits (or losses) of all our labors over the past year. The time we see, in black and white, just how much monetary wealth we accumulated from all those hours at the office, hopefully wise investment choices, and the "moves" we made to avoid giving more than necessary to the U.S. government (you know, Obama 'n 'em).

Now, try helping someone else with their self-worth—in this case, Mom. Her meticulous documentation of charitable donations was especially eye-opening. The old notion of "one man's trash is another man's treasure" really comes in handy when deciding what might have value. Among her list of donations was simply listed "material." When I asked her about this, she explained, "Your father's pants were always too long and needed shortening. I saved those strips of material from the bottoms of all his trousers." "Mom," I said, "you saved all those little strips of material?" "No," she replied, "they were big strips. Someone could make a quilt out of them."

Okay, here are my thoughts:
1. Why would you save those strips of material?
2. Why would you feel the need to donate them?
3. Who would want to make a quilt out of trousers' bottoms?

Oh well, at least there's a little less of Mom's taxes going to the Obama re-election fund...

Lesson Learned: Sometimes the argument is not going to be won. Who's to say what is right or wrong? Save the stress, take a breath, move on to the next one.

Will I Ever Learn My Lesson?

April 2011

Set the Scene: It took Mom a while to agree to get a cell phone, and she never did get a computer because all that "new technology" was simply overwhelming. So, I did my best to help make things easier, but sometimes I needed to put myself in her shoes to understand what she truly needed.

Well, it looks like it's back to basics for me. We laugh when we hear the story about the lady who calls the repairman because her refrigerator isn't working, and he asks, "Is it plugged in?" Yet that is lesson #1— "Don't assume anything."

Mom reported that her cell phone simply wasn't working. She dutifully charged it until the display read "charge complete," but as soon as she took it off the charger, the screen went completely black. Knowing she had bought a new battery just a few months earlier, I thought it best to seek advice from my technology expert (my son). "Sounds like it's more than a battery issue—something is wrong with the phone." We moved the trip to the Verizon store to the top of our to-do list, realizing how necessary a working cell phone is for emergencies.

Handing the phone to the Verizon rep, we explained, "This phone just isn't working." The rep pressed a few buttons and, voilà! Everything was back in working order. "How did you do that?" Mom asked.

"Well," the rep meekly replied, "I just turned it on."

Tail between my legs, I blushed, apologized, and thanked the rep. No use trying to explain this one. Mom's response? "Well, I'm glad I didn't have to put out any more bucks. Let's go to lunch."

Lesson Learned: This one is easy—Don't Assume Anything. Our fast and complicated world demands that we step back and read our audience when trying to share new information. It helps to try to see things from their point of view.

Grandma on Gatorade

August 2011

Set the Scene: Mom was always concerned about her body getting thinner and losing muscle. She often didn't eat much, but she certainly made up for it when presented with some of her favorite foods. She constantly asked the doctor how she could put on weight, though he didn't take it too seriously, since most of his patients were trying to lose weight.

Don't laugh! We were back at the doctor again for the leg that "vibrates." You know what that means: Mom can't go to the gym again! Quite concerned that she would never be able to rebuild her muscles (since she reportedly has "no appetite"), we went out to lunch. Mom consumed half a Captain Morgan's chicken sandwich and most of the sweet potato fries. In fact, since going out to lunch is her favorite pastime, she never ceases to amaze me with her ability to eat an entire loaded baked potato along with half of the O'Charley's rolls and a good portion of a grilled cheese sandwich I wonder what she could eat if she did have an appetite!

Although the previous two courses of Prednisone provided a temporary cure for her leg pain, the doctor was concerned about the long-term effects of prescribing it again. He had an alternate, though unusual, solution: "Try drinking a glass of Gatorade before bedtime." "What flavor?" Mom asked. "You choose the flavor...this works for 1 out of 20 people, so let's see if you might be the one." Excited for the new prospect Mom says, "Did you see the commercial about the kid who offers the teacher a glass of Gatorade...etc, etc, etc." At this point, I'm thinking a Manhattan at lunch might do me some good, too.

So, Mom has once again joined the ranks of athletes, with Gatorade as the solution to her immediate needs. And I may be becoming "older and wiser," learning not to take life so seriously—since simple problems can have simple solutions.

P.S. Did you know... Gatorade contains a lot of the 'trace elements' essential to bodily functions?

Lesson Learned: Just because we may not see an issue as serious doesn't diminish its severity or importance to someone else. It isn't always necessary to "fix" the problem—and sometimes, it can't be fixed—but a simple display of empathy goes a long way in easing someone's burden. And a little patience can ease our own frustration.

A Day with Mom

Oct 2011

Set the Scene: Mom would never part with anything. She was part of the generation that grew up during the Great Depression and, therefore, saw value in everything. So, to avoid breaking Mom's heart, we allowed her to bring all her belongings on the move from Michigan to Cincinnati—including those we saw as "junk." Little by little, we attempted to sort through the piles of "goods."

At the end of the day, if you can remember something that made you smile or laugh, you've had a good day. Today was a very good day. Mom needed to "sort through some things" to make room for the next truckload in the never-ending move from Michigan. This meant she was willing to part with some items that came down on the last move. Here are some highlights from the day:

- In one of the file drawers (you know—the metal file drawer that stays locked), Mom spotted the box for the Belgian waffle maker. Since she declared it hadn't been used since the Dad-days, she convinced me to take it home. However, the box seemed very light, so we opened it—only to find plastic display racks. We have no clue where the waffle maker is, but I'm sure glad those display racks were kept in a safe place.

- Mom has oodles and oodles of cassette tapes that Dad used to play every day. I was quite surprised at how many there were, but she explained, "Your father had those before I met him." I had to put time into perspective for her, reminding her that cassette tapes did not exist in 1956.

- We came across a tote bag (imagine that!). Mom actually agreed to let it go because it was wrinkled... you see, the last time she had a wrinkled tote bag, she tried to iron it, and it disintegrated.

- Ahh...the small white unmarked box. We opened it together with curiosity and anticipation; after all, the contents were wrapped in tissue paper. As we unfolded the paper, Mom proclaimed, "Those were your dad's—they're antiques." "But Mom," I said, "they're dirty, used plastic grill tools."

- And yet another: needing to measure a piece of furniture, Mom grabbed one of her collection of yardsticks. As I watched Mom use it, I noticed it looked peculiar. Somehow, both ends had been cut off. The yardstick began at 4" and ended at $33\frac{1}{2}$". No wonder things aren't fitting like we thought they would.

- But this one took the cake, thanks to our sister Holly. I was feeling a bit discouraged as the movers unloaded multitudes of boxes into the garage. Then came the wardrobe cases (of course containing clothes that had been left in Michigan for the last **2**+ years). I laughed so hard that I made the movers laugh as I read the special note Holly had written on the box: "Important clothes that Mom wears all the time." Thank you, Holly!

And a quote, this one by Benjamin Franklin:
"I conceive that the great part of the miseries of mankind are brought upon them by false estimates they have made of the value of things."

Lesson Learned: What could have been another day of frustration turned into a day of shared laughter. Learning to let the little things go and finding the bright side makes the journey so much simpler.

Which Side of the Coin?

January 2012

Set the Scene: Little by little, as Mom's memory continued slipping, her perspective on life was changing as well. Some of the people and things she once cherished began to annoy her, and she started to see them from a different viewpoint. Fortunately, she was unaware of these changes, which helped keep her spirits up as she viewed the world through her "rose-colored glasses."

Perspective is relative. Spending the day with someone who remembers more about the '30s and '40s than what happened yesterday puts a twist on perspective.

After the morning's test at the hospital, we had to run a few errands…

Passing Dunkin' Donuts, Mom remarked, "I bought some of that Dunkin' Donuts coffee because Bill O'Reilly drinks it. It wasn't so great. Besides, that O'Reilly makes me mad—he's always interrupting people and getting angry. I think he had too much of that Dunkin' Donuts coffee."

Looking down at her arm, Mom saw the hospital bracelet.
"Hey, they have me down here for being 85!"
"That's right, Mom, your birthday was last month."
"No, it wasn't, my birthday is in December."
(Boy, that new calendar at the nursing home must be as bad as Mom said it is.)

On to Target, where we saw many young moms with their small children. Mom was amazed to see these young women with two or three little ones out in the store. "If I were them, I would just stay home." Then she noticed a little girl standing up in the grocery cart. "That one looks too young to even stand. I forgot that people could be so small!!"

Of course, we made a trip to the bakery. After all, Wednesday is Senior Discount Day. Mom bought some sandwiches to take home.

However, she gave me the cookies that came with them because she "doesn't have time for cookies."

It was good to have some laughs. My humor came from seeing things from Mom's point of view. Oh, did I mention that all day long her cell phone kept buzzing? But Mom explained, "They keep calling me to tell me that my battery is low."

Amen! Hallelujah!

Gotta add a quote, this one from Bertrand Russell:

"In all affairs, it's a healthy thing now and then to hang a question mark on the things you have long taken for granted."

Lesson Learned: What's the point in arguing with someone who would struggle to understand any other way or view? Sometimes the purpose of time spent is just that—spending time together. Go with the flow, enjoy the moment, and accept that "the way things are is the way things are."

Lordy, Lordy! Grandma Thinks She's 40!

March 2012

Set the Scene: Mom had been driving Dad's Cadillac DeVille, but as she aged, she was growing shorter and could no longer see over the steering wheel. So, we were on the hunt for a smaller, simpler car. However, Mom was convinced she needed a convertible—like the ones she and Dad had driven together for so many years.

Yep. Hate to break the news, but Grandma seems to be going through a midlife crisis. She's so disheartened that her body just doesn't work like it used to. "These darned doctors aren't fixing the problem." She's struggling to accept such realities as, "I'll never be able to roller skate again," and "I just want to be able to run around the block."

It's not uncommon during these midlife growing pains to want something that makes you feel younger. My son and I picked a sunny day to take Grandma car shopping. Of course, our choices were limited to Ford, since she wouldn't consider owning a foreign-made car and absolutely refuses to deal with any American-made car under Obama's control. I don't think the Ford salesman was prepared when he saw the little 85-year-old lady, her 16-year-old grandson, and me walk into the showroom. He thought he had her figured out at first sight and led her straight to a mid-size luxury car. He realized he was in for something special when she looked at him and said, "That's ugly!"

We strolled—at a snail's pace—around the lot, checking out different options. It gave Mom plenty of time to tell him how she felt about Obama, as well as a good deal about her life story. The salesman kept looking to us for help, so we finally explained, "She really wants a Mustang." His laughter stopped when he saw the excitement on her face. "We only have one on the lot, over there." Who knew that's all it would take to make Mom's leg pain disappear! I'd almost call it skipping—she beat us all over to that black convertible Mustang.

And yet, we're still searching for the perfect car. But my latest concern is, if this is only midlife for Mom, how am I going to keep up with her? I mean, I no longer roller skate or run around the block. I may have to swap my green tea for Manhattans, and my spinach salad for cheeseburgers. It sure seems to work for her!

I'm reminded of what C. S. Lewis said:
"The future is something which everyone reaches at the rate of 60 minutes an hour, whatever he does, whoever he is."

Lesson Learned: A dose of reality is a hard pill to swallow. We can't always convince someone of what we think is best for them; sometimes they have to find out for themselves. A little give and take can lead to a welcome compromise.

P.S. In case you're wondering, she did not buy the Mustang convertible!

Can You Ring Me Up?

September 2012

Set the Scene: Mom was reaching the point where even simple, everyday tasks were becoming complicated.

When did the telephone get added to the list of complicated, "new technology" machines? We're not talking about a cell phone, a smartphone, or even a Bluetooth device, but the basic Alexander Graham Bell telephone. I guess, as we get older, even the ordinary parts of daily living can become a bit overwhelming. I say this because...

Yesterday, I received **three** calls from Mom before noon, each time trying to explain that her phone was not working. She wasn't able to make an outgoing call to my brother. Although I reassured her there was nothing wrong with her phone (since she was able to reach me three times), she took matters into her own hands and called the Operator. Of course, she only got a recording. I can't comment on this because I can't remember the last time I called the Operator.

Now, if you look up the definition of "telephone" on urbandictionary.com, it says:

"What people used in the 1300s and before. The telephone was often used by dinosaurs as a fetch toy. Telephones are like cell phones, only 100 times worse because they are the primitive version. The first person to make a telephone was God's great-grandfather." I'm sure if we asked the grandkids, they would agree.

So, when the world of communication has turned to texting, emailing, and smartphones—and one is only familiar with how to use a "telephone"—you'd better hope the Happy Hour group keeps meeting regularly, so you have at least a little contact with the outside world. Although one might question the quality of communication received from a group of 80-

plus who have all had a few glasses of wine and share the same story they told last month, if they can even remember what last month was!

Lesson Learned: As simple tasks become more difficult, frustration sets in. Being supportive and understanding provides much-needed calmness and reassurance. It's time to delicately step in and help handle the situation without undermining their sense of respect. Working together to solve the issue allows them to feel capable and confident.

Step, Hop, Step, Hop

November 2012

Set the Scene: Back in the day, Mom shopped at the best stores and wore the finest clothing. However, shopping trips were now few and far between, especially since one comes to value the closet full of items collected over the years, and the latest styles seem "ridiculous."

"Everything old is new again." Those are words from some old song—I'm not sure which one, but Mom would know. Yet it perfectly sums up a day at Kenwood Mall with Mom. I heard her repeatedly say, "Oh! There's so much on the market!" referring to the multitude of specialty stores offering plentiful choices of high-priced, questionable-quality items. What happened to getting a new pair of shoes at the start of the school year, or only Santa bringing a much-wanted toy? Then she asked, "Why are there so many cars in the lot—doesn't anybody stay home?"

I tried conscientiously to walk at her pace (step, cane, step, cane) and noticed she looked like a country mouse in the city, in awe of the current styles that didn't make practical sense. Even the sweet aroma of chocolate in the Godiva store couldn't tempt Mom to succumb to even one piece of the overpriced indulgence.

Oh, should I feel guilty or fortunate? I see it like this—it is what it is. We only know what we see around us. We don't often think about where we've come from or where we're going. I learned that from Mom. Today, she met my friend who works with the Alzheimer's group at the nursing home. She told my friend, "I went over there once, but they're just a bunch of old people." So, we see what we want to see.

Lesson Learned: For someone like Mom, who grew up during the Great Depression, thriftiness was a way of life. Our society places too high a value on material things for the sake of image and desire. It's good not to dismiss the thoughts of an old lady—she is right. As I grow older, I appreciate the difference between needs and wants and have more respect for the opinions of those who are "older and wiser."

The Rain in Spain Stay Mainly In The Plain

January 2013

Set the Scene: As Mom's health issues became worse, it was difficult to discern when there was a need for immediate medical attention and simply a need for some comforting sympathy. Always willing to err on the safe side, I offered many times to take her to the hospital or the doctor on call, but she would not have it. She refused to be seen by anyone other than her doctor.

That's a well-known song from a few years back (thank you, Julie Andrews). Mom's version..." the pain, the pain is mainly when the doctor's out". If you remember this song, you're almost as old as I am. Then you would know that the next line goes, "I think he's got it!" For me, the next line is, "I think I've got it!" Meaning, I'm finally catching on to Mom's ways, emotions, and needs.

Seems all the aches and pains are so much more intense on Saturdays, Sundays, and holidays. In other words, when *her* doctor is not available. I've come to learn that somehow Monday mornings ease the pain. Once again, she can walk, drive, socialize; she even mentioned today that she felt like she could ride a horse (!)

I was privileged to attend the annual Christmas gathering of Mom's brothers and sisters, now aged 71-89. A glimpse into our ancestry gave me some comfort as I watched them laugh together, young-hearted and wise. I saw what they share in common – a love for Manhattans and sweets. Each one takes turns boasting proud news of the grandchildren. No complaining, all laughter, sharing old stories; time has not distanced them at all.

We all seek the comfort of family and of something familiar. Whether it's your own doctor, your home, or just a familiar voice on the phone.

Lesson Learned: The aches and pains that come with a failing body are frightening. The reality of what is happening is even more so. Sometimes the best medication is a good listener, a sympathetic voice, a warm hug. We can't expect to understand what they feel, or find a cure, but just being there is invaluable.

Does The End Justify The Means?

April 2013

<u>**Set the Scene:**</u> Mom had moved from Michigan to Cincinnati four years earlier, but fought us long and hard about selling the house. Despite many trips to Michigan to clean out the home and prepare it for the market, Mom was adamant about getting a better price than the current market would offer. It was difficult to convince her that the money she was spending on property tax, home insurance, and repairs for failing items in the vacant house was costing more than the difference in price. She finally agreed to sell, but of course, did not make it easy on us. Her memory was slipping more each day, and confusion over the simplest everyday things was becoming common.

Today, after two and a half hours of scrutiny, Mom signed the contract to list the house in Michigan!!

(A brief pause here, so you can all get a glass of bubbly to raise your hand in a toast.)

So, you're wondering what took two and a half hours? Ha! You should have been there.

Before I arrived, Mom warned me that she had a "horrific" day. Neither one of the TVs was working, which would ruin anyone's day, right? The problem was that Mom was feeling pretty bad about not paying the bill for her supplemental medical insurance, despite three payment warnings, which caused the insurance to lapse. Now, according to Mom, they were "penalizing" her by cutting off her TV service. (Sigh.) She even wondered if they had cut off all her electric service, but I suggested that, since she was talking with me on the landline phone, that probably hadn't happened. A call to the cable company reassured her that this was not part of the "Obama-care" healthcare plan. To make sure she wasn't being victimized, Mom decided to call Suzanne across the street—her Michigan neighbor—to see if her cable was out too. Uh, wrong state...we're in Ohio now.

Finally, on to matters at hand. Never before had I had the opportunity to analyze a legal contract in such depth. But Mom provided many insightful explanations for the property disclosure section:

Q: What year was the house built?

A: Your father and I moved in in 1863.

Q: Does the alarm system work?

A: Every time I make a steak in the broiler.

Q: Are you aware of any lead paint issues?

A: Yes, there is a can of lead-based paint in the small bathroom downstairs.

Needless to say, I left quite concerned. Mom, are you going to be okay with no TV tonight?

"I'll be fine, I'll just play my records on that record player in the kitchen." (Aka Bose CD player)

Well, I was leaving with something good in my hands—a pair of kids' underwear from the American Indian donations (thanks to the many contributions she made to their cause). And a signed contract.

Lesson Learned: Patience on my part had become strained. I was learning to allow extra time to deal with unexpected issues, not just the matter at hand. I struggled with the idea that Mom couldn't comprehend the whys and hows of any given situation. I had to find peace in knowing that I was doing what was best for her and reassure her that everything was going to be okay.

'Tis Good To Laugh At Oneself

June 2013

Set the Scene: Mom had a wonderful sense of humor. She taught us all to laugh at ourselves and to make light of the little things.

Today was a "Mom Day."

It began as usual, sorting through stacks of mail to distinguish junk mail (aka multiple donation requests) from important mail (aka bills due). Then Mom commented, "I got a call confirming a reservation for dinner tonight. I don't remember signing up for any dinner."

Off to lunch. In conversation, Mom mentioned, "You know, I called Pat across the street to see if she signed up for that dinner tonight, but she doesn't know anything about it. Then I called Alice, but she hadn't heard about it either.

On to errands—Target, T.J. Maxx, all the primo spots around town. But Mom was still concerned: "I wonder if someone else signed me up for that dinner. I'll have to call when I get home to see what it's all about."

I was finally back home. Long day, but I thanked my morning cappuccino for the much-needed boost. The phone rang. It was Mom. I could hardly get out "Hi Mom" over the hysterical laughter I heard on the other end...

"Wait 'til you hear this. That dinner tonight is for Alzheimer's. Do you think I need to go? Ha Ha Ha Ha."

An inward smile. It's good to have the ability to see ourselves as we are—and to laugh in spite of it all.

Lesson Learned: Many dementia and Alzheimer's patients are not aware of what is happening to their minds. Those who are aware—who recognize a face but can't put a name to it, or who struggle to find a familiar word—must find it very frustrating. Once again, patience is key. Helping them to help themselves without causing shame or embarrassment helps them maintain self-respect.

A New Car!! A New Day!!

August 2014

Set the Scene: It took a lot of car shopping to find a car small enough for Mom to see out of, and with a dashboard simple enough not to overwhelm the operator. Then, it took quite a bit of convincing to help Mom overcome her feelings of guilt about getting a new car. The tides turned when her grandson landed a summer baseball internship out of town and needed to borrow a car. Mom was absolutely thrilled at the idea of buying a new car so he could use it for the summer! What a giving heart.

We brought home the new car! Thanks to my sister for the ride to the body shop in Amelia. Mom's "new" car looked just like it did the day it first came home. It didn't tell the story of its adventures in Tiffin, Ohio—including the encounter with an unwelcome deer—or its numerous trips to nearby small towns in search of bigger adventures. It now sits in the premium spot in Mom's garage, surrounded by boxes of unknown junk, waiting for its chance to venture out to the hot spots of the community...Kroger! Walgreens! Church! God help it!

As Mom welcomed the new addition, she looked out into the driveway at my Saturn SUV and her Volvo S40 and asked (no kidding!), "Which car is mine?" Seriously, Mom?!

I walked around the old 2000 Caddy, wondering if we'd miss her, and spotted an issue Mom hadn't seen before. The back door on the passenger side had been sideswiped! "I hate going to Kroger," was Mom's reply. I just hoped there wasn't another car out there with silver paint on the bumper...

I decided to take Mom for a ride around the block to show her the ins and outs of the new car. (P.S. Hey, sister—are you still available for driver's training? Please?) Mom's first question: "Do you put the car in Drive before or after you start it?" (Good luck, sister!)

Back to the house—whew! —time to go through the mail stack. "I can't decide if I should buy a ticket for a chance at $10,000. I could use the money for a tax write-off." (Did we go to the same school for accounting 101?)

Then I noticed a new addition to Mom's treasure collection: a baseball, signed and in a special case, holding a front-row seat on Mom's entry table. "Mom, this is really cool! What is it?" Mom replied, "It's a baseball, signed by a pro." I looked closely. The signature was clearly her grandson Tyler's, thanking her for the use of her car all summer. Wow! That truly is something special—a baseball signed by a pro! Thanks, Tyler, for helping to put everything into perspective.

Lesson Learned: Sometimes, we think the best way to help someone is by giving them what they want. Mom was at a point where no car would have been better than any new car. But taking away the keys—aka taking away her independence—was a much bigger battle. The time for "tough love" is when we put someone's safety first, even if that means they will be angry with us. Mom did that for us when we were young, and it's time for us to do the same for her. Luckily, Mom let me do the driving when we went out...

Let It Go, Let It Go

Sep 2014

Set the Scene: Mom and Dad were avid Cadillac fans, partly because it was American-made and partly because it represented the US union workers, to which Dad had belonged. Although the "Caddy" was much too large for Mom to drive, it was one more memory of Dad that she could not relinquish.

That's the granddaughter's favorite song, from the movie Frozen. Yet, I was singing that song over and over in my head today as I followed Mom, driving the Caddy, to turn it over to its new owner. I had already spent the afternoon in the garage, going through those infamous boxes of "who knows what," repeating, "just throw it away – let it go." But now, it was time to let go of the car that carried memories of 14 years of trips back and forth to Michigan. The car that Dad chose to drive was so representative of the union automakers of the Detroit-Lansing area. The car that Mom chose to drive because Dad drove it first. The car that the youngest grandson drove when he first got his license, which turned out to be a pretty sweet ride for a 16-year-old, with room for many passengers and some nice amenities to boot. The car that the son-in-law was proud enough to drive, as coach, to his son's football games.

It did not matter that all four corners had a story to tell – black skid marks on the front left, a dent in the rear right, and so on. Not to mention the new side-swiped indentation on the passenger side rear door. Beat up as she may have seemed, she carried so much history and stories in her short 14 years. I surprised myself as I questioned whether we were doing the right thing in passing her on. But yesterday's flat tire gave the needed affirmation that the poor old girl was running down. Time to move on. As I followed the 2000 Cadillac Deville down the street, it looked like a different car already...I did not see the pink stuffed pig suction-cupped to the back window from Dad. There were no mid-century cassette tapes in the console. And no one was going to valet park this car at a corporate convention.

But since she still wore her decal to show support for the Michigan police, I knew she would be okay.

Lesson Learned: Sometimes it's hard for us to understand someone else's attachment to a certain thing. However, when those memories are also our memories, we see things in a different light. Try to see things from their perspective to understand what is important to them. We never want to diminish their feelings or emotions. Our memories become increasingly precious as we age.

Groceries With Grandma

Feb 2015

<u>**Set the Scene:**</u> A trip to the grocery store was a social outing for Mom, since she now had to rely on others to take her out. Lingering over decisions on what to buy, and moving very slowly up and down the aisles to see all that was offered, were ways of procrastinating the return home. Now, if we could only teach her how to drive the motorized shopping cart!

The day begins with - you guessed it - lunch.
Next stop - the liquor store. That explains a lot.

Mom has come to accept that every trip to the grocery means a ride in the electric cart. I drop Mom off to park the car. When I enter Kroger, she has multiple store clerks assisting her with finding a cart that is charged and ready to go. They are relieved as they see me approaching.

I have learned that we must begin our shopping trip in the liquor aisle. No reason to waste time going up and down the bread and soup aisles, as Mom will repeatedly ask, "Do they have the Vermouth in this aisle?" It's simply a matter of priorities. I cannot venture too far since I have to help steer the electric cart as it is heading straight towards the display of wine bottles, with its driver looking sideways, trying to decide where she wants to go.

Next aisle – frozen foods. Mom stocks up. But it must be on sale. For some reason, it is acceptable to spend $20 for two on lunch for sandwiches and coffees, but frozen dinners cannot exceed $2.50.

Now we can really move. We zip past the household cleaning aisle and the fresh meat section because, well, who needs that? A teenage boy, lazily slumped over the meat case, looks curiously at the little old lady in the red coat approaching him in the electric cart, her cane hanging on the side. But wow! Can he pick up his pace and move quickly when he realizes that she is NOT going to stop!

We slow down as we enter the candy and cookie aisle. I have learned the only way to deal with this display of heavenly goodies is to find some product that Mom likes further down the aisle, such as chocolate-covered pretzels, and holding them up in the air, say, "Hey Mom, aren't these what you're looking for?"

I realize we have been in the grocery store for a while. I'm sure I have reached my 10,000 steps. I must sneak-eat a protein energy bar to keep going, but I must make sure Mom does not see me to avoid the inevitable 20 minutes of examining health bars, none of which she can eat because of her teeth.

Mom spies the tomatoes and says, "Boy, those look good." I choose one and ask, "Do you like Roma's?" Mom wants to feel it. Then she wants to feel the organic tomato. Then she wants to feel the vine-ripened tomatoes, the one on top. "Which one would you like, Mom?"

She replies, "It doesn't matter, they're all the same."

We finally check out, but Mom always insists on going in her own separate checkout lane. As I go back to collect her, I mouth to the cashier, "Thank you!" She says, "No problem. By the way, she has some cream puffs that she is going to share with you." I have to smile. What else did Mom tell her?

Mom insists on driving the electric cart out to the car. My heart races as we play dodge-ems in the parking lot with drivers looking for parking spots, not paying attention to us. The only problem is, once Mom is inside my car, I have to return the electric cart. The only way it will operate is for me to ride it back. Shame on those people staring at me – they have no idea!

Yes, Grandma is 88 and doing pretty great. Me? Oh, I have 88 bottles of beer on the wall. I'm fine.

Lesson Learned: We have to slow down! The time we give to our loved ones is so very precious to them. Our lives are busy and hurried, we feel pulled in so many directions, and can never seem to get everything done. Carving out uninterrupted time as a caregiver is one of the many difficulties we face, but one we will never regret.

It's Good to be Back

Sep 2015

Set the Scene: Mom loved watching the news, and it had better be Fox News! She had an opinion on everything, and there was no letting down. However, her understanding of what was taking place in the news was diminishing.

My son and I had lunch with Mom today, which included... alas!!... a few laughs! Maybe putting on those 5 pounds has lifted Mom's spirits. The ol' girl was back, including her viewpoints on what's happening in the news...

"Why are they picking on that football player because of his deflated balls? Why don't they deflate all the balls and let everyone play under the same premise?!" (Reference – Tom Brady)

"What about that girl making all the news running around with no clothes on??" (Reference – Miley Cyrus)

We went back to the cottage to do some laundry and wash the bed sheets. When Mom said, "I miss doing laundry!" I had to wonder if we were related. However, she redeemed herself by sharing her theory on washing sheets: "I sleep on one side of the bed for a week, then on the other side the next week, so I only have to change sheets every two weeks."

Okay, so she does have an opinion or theory for any given subject. But I'll bet she would 100% agree with this quote from Bill O'Reilly: "The country is a better place because Fox News has succeeded."

Lesson Learned: When the light and funny times are farther and fewer between, we have to take advantage of them. No reason to argue with someone's point of view who would struggle to communicate their thoughts. Let the good times roll!

The Truth Serum

Jan 2016

Set the scene: Mom had reached the point of confusing times, places, and things. I often had to think outside the box to interpret what she was trying to tell me or what her needs were. Now add a glass of wine to that mix...

Alcohol has been known to be called "truth serum," perhaps because it brings out the "real" person, or perhaps because it causes people to speak the truth. Did I hear someone say, "uh oh... oh no"? Well, you're right there.

I visited Mom late Friday afternoon because she wanted me to look over some papers that came in the mail. Turns out they were from the accountant to prepare for last year's taxes. After helping Mom understand, "Why do I have to pay this guy every year?" I told her to be on the lookout for any 1099s that might come in the mail. "Oh, I'm getting those already." Hmmm. Since the "2015 Tax" folder was empty,

I asked her where they were. She pulled out her copy of the Western Hills Pink Pages (local phone book), and there, tucked neatly under the "P's," was her 1099 for Social Security. She explained that she placed them next to "Parkway Dry Cleaners" because they do her taxes every year. Sounds like there's going to be a scavenger hunt at Mom's for tax papers this year.

Mom decided she could use a change of pace from the retirement hall dining room, so we treated ourselves to a dinner out in town. We allowed ourselves each a glass of red wine. After all, it was the weekend. A little wine brings on a lot of talk. Mom talked on and on about the wonderful Bill O'Reilly. She was sure that, although he was smart as a whip on those politics, she might have voted before him since she believed she cast her first vote at 16. That meant, at least to Mom, that she had one leg up on him when it came to politics. However, she was convinced they were both in their 80s. "Mom, do you want to know how old Bill O'Reilly really is? He's 66!" Mom said that my computer had to be wrong. I had to explain, in super-brief format, how the internet worked. Mom was a little disappointed until she realized, "Well then, I did vote before him!" Then I realized it… "Grandma has a cru-ush. Grandma has a crush." Wait! That makes Grandma a cougar! Let's move on….

But not away from politics! She turned to bashing Hillary Clinton. "She's only running for office to spite her husband for having that affair. He might be out screwing around, but he's a lot smarter than she is!"

Alas! I was saved by the host at the restaurant. He approached me and asked, "Don't I know you from the Dew Drop Inn?" Now I've been to a few bars on the west side, but never the Dew Drop Inn. I smiled and assured him that he must have me confused with someone else. That brought lots of arm-nudging from Mom, with the voice of a kid on a school playground, saying, "Oh yeah, you know him from the Dew

Drop Inn. You probably had a one-night stand and just don't remember it."!! Mom!!

There's probably so much more to the ol' gal that we still have yet to learn. Who knows what happened those 31 years before we started coming around? Or even those nights Mom and Dad snuck out to the Moon Cafe? Maybe we need to bring back those Happy Hours and call them "History Class." Who's down?

Lesson Learned: Sometimes we need to remember that our parents had lives before we were born. They spent most of their adult lives acting as role models, parenting, and being responsible. I'm sure it felt good for Mom to let her guard down and share some good laughs.

White or Rye?

April 2016

Set the Scene: As Mom's dementia progressed, she became feisty and argumentative. Balancing the new challenges along with my own life became more difficult and often frustrating. It became more important to keep my perspective focused on what was most important.

I realize that I'm a perfect example of the "sandwich generation," but I often wonder which sandwich I am. Recently, I've been thinking about meatloaf, because sometimes it's good, and sometimes you don't even want to touch it. Balancing parents, kids, grandkids, along with a house and career, truly gives one a wide perspective on life.

Today, Mom had me thinking I might be more of a Limburger cheese sandwich. She was being her usual feisty self until I told her, in an attempt to change the subject, about my friend's father who had just passed away.

"How old was he?"

"90."

"Oh, well, he probably died of old age." … "How old am I, 89 or 90?"

"Mom, you're 89. You don't turn 90 until December."

"So, I'm 89 until I turn 90?"

(Help me with this one!) "Ummm, yeah."

For some reason, that was acceptable. But, after lunch, we had to go to Target to buy wrinkle cream.

Yet the day before, I spent time with a couple of amazing little people. My 2-year-old grandson had no inhibitions as he jammed down alone in front of the TV, trying to mimic the Elvis impersonator. The 7-year-old granddaughter had her own unique way of seeing things… as her mother was reading her a book about seahorses, she said, "I thought sea horses were big like earth horses." Her mother reminded her that she had seen the seahorses at the aquarium. "Ahhhh," she said, "I thought those were the babies!"

Whether they're almost eight or almost 90, they all make me laugh. They help me to see life from so many different views than just my crazed middle-aged life. They remind me that we came into the world with no inhibitions and eventually reach an age where we leave the inhibitions behind. And that we should take ourselves more lightly and not worry about the small stuff.

I think I'm going to be more like a peanut-butter-and-jelly sandwich, because doesn't everybody like a good old PB and J?

Lesson Learned: Balancing life, family, and career as a caregiver is one of our greatest challenges. We are the ones who need to change our priorities to make room for everyone else who needs us. So, we need to take a step back and make the best of it all. Take a breath, look at the light side, and find the laughter. We need to do a lot of giving, but we are getting back so much more!

Great Grandmother, Great Granddaughter, Great Scott!

Aug 2016

Set the Scene: Mom was now living at the retirement center in assisted living. Today I took my 7-year-old granddaughter, Layla, to visit her great-grandmother for lunch in the dining room. It was such a welcome and humorous break for me…. They shared a conversation that lacked logic, but which they both seemed to enjoy. Their many laughs together amused me and brought them closer together.

Layla joined me on a visit to see Mom this afternoon. We found her in the dining room with what looked like every choice on the menu in front of her, which she explained was making up for missing breakfast and lunch.

As I sat across the table from Mom and Layla, I realized my best vantage point was to be the observer. I was touched and amused at the conversation that spanned an 82-year age difference, three generations, and a lot of "Layla – philosophy."

Mom: "There goes that man singing his old songs out loud again."

Layla: "I'll bet these people talk about when they were young all the time, because they miss being young." (Amazingly insightful for 7!)

Mom: "Look – that man over there just celebrated his 100th birthday!"

Layla: "Some people live to be 100, some don't. It's just a fact of life."

Mom: "I'm stuck here all the time."

Layla: "I feel bad that you can't get out. All you do is stay inside and do boring stuff."

Mom: (After Layla made some comment about me...) "Boy, you've got her number!"

Layla: "No, I don't know her number; I'm not old enough."

Mom: "That lady behind me is 95 years old, and always forgets that she has already eaten."

Layla: "At least she's not dying."

Mom: "That nurse is the bull in a china shop!"

Layla: "What?! She's Chinese?"

I cannot make this stuff up. In fact, I could not write down notes fast enough! Most importantly, they both enjoyed themselves. Layla had blackberry cobbler and ice cream for dinner because Great-Grandma said she could.

"Great Scott! Mystery upon mystery, and marvel upon marvel!" (Bet you didn't know that saying originated in the Eclectic Medical Journal, 1856)

Lesson Learned: With time, I learned that I didn't always need to "fix things." What had become most important to Mom was visits from family. She was going to eat whatever she wanted to eat, do what she wanted to do on her terms, and felt it appropriate to state her feelings without regard to whom she might offend. Keeping Mom happy was my main priority at this point. And if that was as simple as a visit from family, then let's make that happen!

The Best Laid Plans...

September 2017

Set the Scene: It has been quite a while since the last entry. Mom's health declined rapidly, reaching the point where she could no longer live safely on her own. We had to make the move to the skilled nursing unit — with more arguments and tough love than I can recount here. Yet, as always, she quickly made new friends and continued insisting on doing everything herself, no matter how difficult it became. My role shifted to Head of the Clean-Up Committee—secretly fixing the problems created by this strong-willed woman while trying to help her maintain her dignity.

Try as we might, Mom just isn't going to let anybody do anything she doesn't want done. That includes the best nurses, the repairmen, the folks at the bank, Bill O'Reilly, the Pope, or any of her 19 "perfect" children, grandchildren, or great-grandchildren. "So, help me God!" as Mom would say.

In fact, Mom is now taking on Mother Nature herself, determined to turn this aging process around in another direction. It doesn't matter what the "higher-ups" have planned for her—she thinks she can beat that, too. I mean, seriously, why would a 90-year-old woman need someone to show her how to work her new wheelchair? Who in the heck thought a personal aide to help her get out of bed those mornings when she "can't walk across the floor" was a good idea? And why on earth would anyone dare think she needs new clothes when there are plenty of perfectly good clothes in the file cabinet, stacked in cardboard boxes under the files, and buried beneath piles of paper?

In spite of Mom's good-heartedness and willingness to help anyone who needs it, she made those poor aides sit out in the hall and refused to let them in to help her. Really! Can you imagine? They were trying to help her get dressed—something she has done herself for 90 years! Who needs them?!

So, the aides have been cancelled. The clothes are all being returned. And Mom is having races in her new wheelchair. The upside, you ask? Mom is so determined not to take help that she is now getting up, dressed, and out and about—which, at the end of the day, was worth it all. Unintended consequences, in a good sort of way.

But the highlight, at least for me, is when Mom introduces me (for the 50th time) to one of the many friends she has made, and they look up and smile and say, "Your Mom is a gem!"

As I left Mom today, she was going to read the newspaper and wait until the dining room opened for dinner. She let me in on their little trick—they all hide the shared newspapers in the top drawer so no one will throw them away. There's nothing wrong with reading yesterday's news since no one over there knows what day it is anyway! I left with a bagful of articles Mom had clipped from those shared newspapers, but I won't tell anyone...

Lesson Learned: For our mom, independence was the last thing she was willing to give up. Her will to keep going was truly what kept her going, and cleaning up after the messes was a small price to pay to see her fighting spirit carry on.

Mom

January 2018

Set the Scene: Mom passed away this month. Her COPD, coupled with dementia, took away her ability to fight any longer. Mom fought the good fight—she finished the race and kept the faith.

There is no greater gift than to have someone so special in your life who helps you realize the kind of person you want to become, as well as opens your eyes to the goodness in others. Someone who can see all that life has to offer and reaches out to take hold of every bit of it—and then shares it with you—someone who thrives on giving to others, putting someone else's needs ahead of their own.

How blessed to be taught that we are all equals, and that each of us has the opportunity to create the life we want by finding in ourselves the gumption and will to make it happen. To find the fun in any situation and always have a reason to laugh. And that is when you find the person who is your best friend and true-life partner, you stand by their side through thick and thin and never let them go.

How fortunate to be praised for our strengths and forgiven for our shortcomings. To be shown how to endure whatever challenges life presents and make the best of them. And that family comes first because love and caring begin at home and then spread to those around us.

Mom was truly our precious gift. She has passed on to us the wisdom and heart to spread that joy of life, that courage to endure, and that spirit to live life to the fullest—to our children and to anyone we meet who might need a piece of Mom's heart.

www.ingramcontent.com/pod-product-compliance
Lightning Source LLC
Chambersburg PA
CBHW061801070526
44586CB00023B/2664